FORGIVENESS

J. Marsden

D1513051

10 Publishing
a division of 10 of those.com

Published by 10Publishing, a division of 10ofthose.com
Ten Of Those Ltd, Unit C Tomlinson Road Leyland PR25 2DY

Email: info@10ofthose.com

Website: www.10ofthose.com

ISBN 978-1-909611-63-4

Designed by Mike Thorpe
www.design-chapel.com

Printed and bound by CPI Group (UK) Ltd, Croydon, CR0 4YY

Reprinted 2016

Contents

5

Why Forgiveness Matters

9

How Sin Affects Relationships

12

Getting Some Things Clear

15

Jesus Teaches Forgiveness

19

Truths about Forgiveness

31

How Jesus' Story Helps Us to Forgive

36

But Where is the Justice?

39

Know Your Job

41

Thinking Personally

45

Two Final Thoughts . . .

Why Forgiveness Matters

Years ago, I worked in a primary school. One break-time in the staff room, the chat turned to something which had happened a number of years before. It seemed that the head had put in a very unpopular policy without consulting anyone. It was news to me – it was before my time. But one of the senior staff who had been there said these words about what had happened: 'I will never forgive him for that – never.' It was a remarkable moment for me, for suddenly I knew why so many things about the school were as they were. Relationships, atmospheres, dynamics in meetings and all sorts of things had been soured and spoilt. The consequences of that person's decision not to forgive were everywhere in that school so many years later. Perhaps you know of similar situations.

Forgiveness is an issue for all of us. All of us live amongst sinners every day, so all of us are sinned against, not once but many, many times. We ourselves are sinners too, so we wrong others repeatedly as well. Sin damages relationships, and when people wrong us, strong reactions and emotions rise up in our hearts.

When people wrong us, strong reactions and emotions rise up in our hearts

Some of us may be carrying very deep wounds from particular events in the past. You may be living now in challenging situations, perhaps in marriages and families, where you have to forgive the same sin over and over again. It is so easy to hold grudges and to want to hurt back. How should we respond when people wrong us?

Jesus Christ spoke compellingly about forgiveness. After His death and resurrection, He told His followers that 'repentance and forgiveness of sins [would] be preached in his name to all nations' (Luke 24:47). That is glorious good news. Jesus died to pay for our sins and bring us free forgiveness. This forgiveness from God is now available to all who repent and trust Christ.

God forgives us through Christ. And we are called to become, in our turn, people who forgive. Over and over again in the New Testament, Christians are reminded that God has forgiven all their sins through Christ's death. And time and again, too, Christians are commanded to forgive.

So, Paul writes to the Christians in Colossae, 'forgive

whatever grievances you may have against one another. Forgive as the Lord forgave you' (Col. 3:13, my italics).

In the Lord's Prayer, Jesus taught His followers to pray, 'Forgive us our sins, *for we also forgive everyone who sins against us*' (Luke 11:4, my italics).

Forgiveness can seem very hard. Sometimes it can seem quite beyond us. We need God to help us and we need to prayerfully seek His help.

But however hard it may seem, we need to be clear that forgiving people is not an optional extra in the Christian life. It is like the litmus test of being a Christian. It is not that forgiving others is something we do to earn God's forgiveness. But forgiving those who wrong us is a sign of the genuineness of our new life in Christ.

> Forgiving people is not an optional extra

There are a number of stark warnings in Scripture that to refuse to forgive is to declare yourself outside of Christ and His forgiveness. Jesus said, 'if you do not forgive men their sins, your Father will not forgive your sins' (Matt. 6:15).

So, we are on very serious ground here. We cannot just dismiss Jesus' command to forgive as being too difficult for us. Jesus is clear. If we refuse to forgive those who wrong us, we will not receive forgiveness from God ourselves. And to face God unforgiven is a truly terrible prospect. It means that we will have to pay for our sins ourselves and will face a lost eternity. Yes, this is very serious ground.

But we have many questions about forgiveness.

What does forgiveness actually look like in practice? It's important I know so I can be clear if I have done it or not.

- Does forgiving someone mean I must drop all criminal charges against that person?

- I still feel angry about what happened. Does that mean I haven't forgiven that person?

- What if the other person is not sorry about what happened? What then?

- Does forgiveness mean that I must treat that other person exactly as if the sin never happened?

- And what about when I just don't want to forgive, or I feel I can't forgive? What then?

We have all sorts of questions.

In coming to understand forgiveness, it's helpful to think first about what happens when someone wrongs another person.

Questions to think about and discuss …

- **What effects does sin have in personal relationships?**

- **How do people tend to react when they have been wronged?**

How Sin Affects Relationships

Sin has so many consequences. Our first reactions to being wronged are often pain and anger.

Someone wrongs us and we experience *pain*. It may be physical pain; it will certainly be emotional pain. We are wronged, and emotionally we may feel as if we have been punched in the stomach. We may also feel *angry*. The wrongness of what has been done to us may provoke a sense of anger, of outrage. 'How could you do that to me?!' 'That is just *so* wrong!'

And the closer we are to the other person, the more intense that pain and anger will tend to be. For example, if my husband lies to me, it will hurt much more than if I am conned by someone cold-calling me on the phone.

So, our first reactions tend to be pain and anger. What is likely to happen next?

Let me mention four things which I have observed in others or seen in myself.

First, *payback*.

There can be a desire to make the other person pay for what they have done in some way.

If you say something hurtful to me, I will want to say something hurtful back. I want you to experience the pain I have experienced, because I think you deserve it. And if I don't say it out loud, I will say it to you in my mind. Or I will file what has happened and wait for an opportunity to pay you back. And if something bad happens to you, I may be secretly pleased because you are getting payback, and I think you deserve it.

Then secondly, there is the *divide* that sin causes in relationships.

You wrong me, and I will want to put distance between you and me. It may be physical distance. It will certainly be emotional distance. That is partly me protecting myself from more pain. But in its own way, this divide is payback, too. For sin breaks relationships, either by starting a fight or by causing a rift, a division. Either way, the relationship is spoiled.

Sin breaks Relationships, either by starting a fight or by causing a rift, a division

Thirdly, there is what we might call the *playback loop*.

Very often the wrong done in the past lives on in the present in our minds. It's as if a record of what happened is stored on a film, and the film keeps playing back over and over again in our minds.

Lastly, there is the cancer of *bitterness* which will grow in our hearts if we nurture and feed a grudge.

Replaying the film of how we were wronged again and again in our minds can lead to very damaging consequences. Very often we end up fanning the flames of bitterness, which may have begun as only sparks smouldering in our hearts. As we dwell again and again on the wrongness of what has been done to us, we can find ourselves stoking the flames of resentment and bitterness

How hard it is to stop feeding and nursing a grudge

so that they blaze fiercer and fiercer. And in time, a lethal forest fire of bitterness will rage in our hearts. This growing bitterness can twist and damage us inside as little else can. Such bitterness often does not stay in a small compartment of our lives. It can colour our whole character and all our relationships. And yet, how hard it is to stop feeding and nursing a grudge.

And into all these reactions and emotions, Jesus says, 'Forgive.' What does that mean?

Getting Some Things Clear

The first thing we need to be clear on is that this call to forgive is speaking about what goes on in our hearts as we respond within personal relationships.

The Bible makes a distinction between how we are to respond to sin in terms of personal relationships and how sin is to be dealt with externally within society, both society as a whole and also inside distinct groups within society. Such groups include local churches and individual families.

In families, in local churches and in our wider society, certain people have a delegated authority from God to administer punishments to those who do wrong.

Paul writes that human 'governing authorities' have been 'established by God', and that the person in authority is 'God's servant, an agent of wrath to bring punishment on the wrongdoer' (Rom. 13:1,4). Today, the police, the courts and the prison authorities all act on behalf of our government in different ways to punish those who do wrong. All these roles have a delegated authority from God.

Parents too have a delegated authority from God over their children, and church leaders over their congregations. 'Children, obey your parents,' writes Paul in Colossians 3:20. And the author of Hebrews writes to Christian churches, 'Obey your leaders and submit to their authority' (Heb. 13:17).

This delegated authority is to be exercised in different ways in different contexts, but people in *all* these roles have a responsibility to show that wrongdoing must be punished. And they are to administer punishments – for discipline, for training and for the protection of others.

Authorities are to administer punishments

However, we do need to be clear that none of these human authorities can fully and finally deal with sin. No one is going to stand before God on the last day and say, 'I'm in the clear with you, God, because I have done my time in Wormwood Scrubs prison.'

But these authorities are still to administer human justice

now and it is right that we help them in this. So, for example, if you are attacked and robbed, it is right for you to cooperate with the police and the courts to bring the criminal to justice. That, again, is a separate issue from forgiveness. Forgiveness does not mean that there are no consequences now for that person's actions. That person may go to prison.

There may be consequences within personal relationships, too. Forgiveness does not mean that you must treat an offender exactly as if the offence had never taken place. It may not be wise to treat the person in exactly the same way as you did before – maybe for their good, or for your protection.

For example, it would not be wise to put someone struggling with a gambling addiction in charge of the church petty cash. And it would be extremely unwise to ask someone who has been convicted of child abuse to be your babysitter. Those kind of decisions are, again, something separate from forgiveness. Forgiveness is about what happens in my heart and in my personal response to the other person.

Forgiveness is about what happens in my heart

Jesus Teaches Forgiveness

So what *is* forgiveness? To help us understand exactly what forgiveness is, we'll look at a famous parable Jesus told His followers about forgiveness. The parable is found in Matthew 18 verses 21 to 35.

The context of this story is Jesus' teaching about how the church is to respond when Christians sin against one another. For, of course, everyone in the church remains a sinner. But the question is, will sin blow apart relationships in Jesus' family, just like it does everywhere else? What should you do when 'your brother' sins against you? Because he will. To be frank, it's only a matter of time. What should you do?

Jesus begins to answer this question in the earlier part of this chapter, in verses 15 to 20. His answer is that first you must make every effort to bring your brother to repentance. It is vital that your brother does repent, for only then can he receive forgiveness from God, and also from you.

So, if your brother sins against you, you are to go to him privately and show him his fault. The aim here is not to humiliate your brother or to crow over his mistakes. The aim is change. You want your brother to recognize his sin and turn from it so that he can receive forgiveness. You want your brother to listen to you. You want to win him over because he is in great danger spiritually.

If he won't listen to a private word, you must bring others in to help, first just a few and then finally, if needs be, the whole church. You are to make every, *every* effort to help your brother take heed and repent of his sin, so that he can receive forgiveness and fellowship can be restored.

Peter's mind seems to be whirring at this point. It is as if he is thinking, 'But suppose my sinning brother *does* repent? And then sins again and repents again? And then sins *again* and repents again? And again and again? What then? There must be limits, Lord? Limits to this forgiveness business? You must reach a point when you say, "That's it! That is just too much now. I am not forgiving that"?'

And in verse 22 Jesus responds. Here is Jesus' word to us for the times we feel we just can't do it any more.

Matthew 18:21-35

Then Peter came to Jesus and asked, 'Lord, how many times shall I forgive my brother [or sister who] sins against me? Up to seven times?'

Jesus answered, 'I tell you, not seven times, but seventy-seven times.

'Therefore, the kingdom of heaven is like a king who wanted to settle accounts with his servants. As he began the settlement, a man who owed him ten thousand talents was brought to him. Since he was not able to pay, the master ordered that he and his wife and his children and all that he had be sold to repay the debt.

'The servant fell on his knees before him. "Be patient with me," he begged, "and I will pay back everything." The servant's master took pity on him, cancelled the debt and let him go.

'But when that servant went out, he found one of his fellow-servants who owed him a hundred denarii. He grabbed him and began to choke him. "Pay back what you owe me!" he demanded.

'His fellow-servant fell to his knees and begged him, "Be patient with me, and I will pay you back."

'But he refused. Instead, he went off and had the man thrown into prison until he could pay the debt. When the other servants saw what had happened, they were greatly distressed and went and told their master everything that had happened.

'Then the master called the servant in. "You wicked servant," he said, "I cancelled all that debt of yours because you begged me to. Shouldn't you have had mercy on your fellow-servant just as I had on you?" In anger his master handed him over to the jailers to be tortured, until he should pay back all he owed.

'This is how my heavenly Father will treat each of you unless you forgive your brother [or sister] from your heart.'

A question to think about and discuss . . .
• **What do we learn in this passage about forgiveness?**

Truths about Forgiveness

God's Word has much to teach us about forgiveness. As we read Jesus' story here, we see Jesus showing us five great truths about forgiveness.

In Jesus' story, the king represents God. The servants are Christians. The first servant is a Christian who has been wronged, the second is the one who has wronged him and who is now seeking his forgiveness. So what can we learn here about forgiveness?

1. Forgiveness means it's over. The debt which is owed is cancelled.

In the story, the first servant owes the king a great debt – millions and millions of pounds in today's money. It is a real tangible mountain of money which needs to be paid back. The servant is facing ruin. What happens? Look at verse 27. The king cancels the debt and lets him go. Just like that. It's as if the king rips the page out of his account book. It's gone. Debt? What debt? It's over.

And that is what forgiveness is like. Sin creates something like a debt between two people. You wrong me and there is this problem between us. Forgiveness is when I say in my heart, 'It's over. I am going to rip out the page. I am going to stop holding that on record. There is going to be clean air between us.'

That is what happens when God forgives us. Paul writes about this experience of receiving God's forgiveness in Romans chapter 4.

'Blessed are they whose transgressions are forgiven, whose sins are covered. Blessed is the man whose sin the Lord will never count against him' (Rom. 4:7–8).

Blessed is the man, blessed is the woman, whose sin the Lord will *never* count against them. What wonderful words! How blessed is the person whose sin the Lord will never count against them. When God forgives us, it's over. And it's over for ever.

How blessed is the person whose sin the Lord will never count against them

And that is how we too are to forgive.

In Mark's Gospel, Jesus contrasts holding something against someone with forgiving them. Jesus says, 'if you hold anything against anyone, forgive him' (Mark 11:25).

Forgiveness means that you let go of the file of that person's sin. You stop holding on to it. You stop holding it against them. It's over.

2. Forgiveness is pure grace. It is totally undeserved.

Forgiveness is totally undeserved. That is the point.

Sometimes when we are wronged, we scratch around for reasons why the person sinned. We are trying to find reasons to excuse them. 'They were stressed', 'They had a bad childhood' or whatever.

Or we try to look for good things to balance out the bad. We are trying to make it easier to forgive them, to feel somehow that they deserve it.

But if you earn it or deserve it, that is not forgiveness, that is justice. That is just getting what is rightfully yours. Forgiveness looks sin full in the face, calls it 'sin' and says, 'It's over.' It is giving someone mercy, not justice.

Look at verse 27 of Jesus' story in Matthew 18. The king 'took pity' on his sinful undeserving servant. He had mercy on him (v. 33). Forgiveness is pure grace. The person doesn't deserve it. That is the point.

And because of this, there are no limits to forgiveness. You never reach a point where you can say, 'That's too much, now. That person does not deserve to be forgiven any more.' If they *deserved* to be forgiven, it wouldn't be forgiveness.

Jesus told Peter that he must forgive 'seventy-seven times' or 'seventy times seven', which is Jesus' way of saying infinity, no limits. That is how God forgives us. God never says, 'Oh-oh, that's once too often now. That's *it*! No more forgiveness for *you*.' And that is how we are to keep forgiving, too.

3. Forgiveness is a two-sided transaction. It takes two to complete it.

Forgiveness is like giving someone a gift, or giving someone my hand in friendship. I can offer it. I can put out my hand to you. But if you don't receive it, if you don't put out your hand to accept mine, there is a sense in which forgiveness remains only half done.

We read in the book of Acts that God's forgiveness is something which is both given and received.

'God exalted [Jesus] to his own right hand as Prince and Saviour that he might *give* repentance and *forgiveness* of sins to Israel' (Acts 5:31, my italics).

'All the prophets testify about [Jesus] that everyone who believes in him *receives forgiveness* of sins through his name' (Acts 10:43, my italics).

Forgiveness is given and forgiveness is received – forgiveness is a transaction which has two sides.

And forgiveness *can only be received with repentance.* Forgiveness can only be received if there is an acknowledgement that wrong has been done and that forgiveness is needed.

For example, suppose you had stolen from me and I said to you, 'I forgive you for stealing all that money from my house last Thursday.' What would you say? Would you say, 'I never stole any money from you! I can't believe you would suggest such a thing.'? Or would you say, 'Thank you, thank you so much for forgiving me. I have been feeling just awful about taking that money!'? Do you see? Accepting forgiveness involves acknowledging guilt.

That is true with receiving God's forgiveness. And it is true with our forgiveness of each other, too. That is why Jesus is at such pains to tell us earlier in Matthew 18 how to help each other come to repentance. Because the person who has sinned does need to repent if they are to receive forgiveness and have a restored relationship.

> The person who has sinned does need to repent if they are to receive forgiveness

Jesus says in Luke 17:3: 'If your brother sins, rebuke him, and if he repents, forgive him.' Do you see the 'if' there? '. . . *if* he repents, forgive him' (my italics). I don't think Jesus means, 'If he doesn't repent, make sure you harbour the bitterest grudge you can muster and go all out for revenge.' No. I think Jesus is just saying that if your brother refuses to repent, the full transaction of forgiveness can't be completed. Apologies that need to be made and accepted remain unsaid. You can and you should offer forgiveness, but the other person needs to repent and receive it. Otherwise the two-sided transaction of forgiveness remains in some sense incomplete. It is like putting out your hand to someone who doesn't respond.

You can put out your hand, you can offer forgiveness. But you can only do your half of what is needed to restore the relationship. Forgiveness needs to be both given and received to reach its final goal. Your brother needs to acknowledge his sin, repent of it and accept the forgiveness you are offering. Only then can the relationship be properly restored.

> Forgiveness needs to be both given and received to reach its final goal

It is perhaps worth saying here that we need to be very careful that we distinguish between what is sin and what is not. I need to be very clear that my brother *has* actually sinned against me before I set off to try, humbly and gently, to show him his fault.

Has my brother sinned against me, or am I just in an irritable, grumpy, oversensitive frame of mind? Have I misinterpreted his actions or his motives? Am I just being touchy?

I have noticed over the years that some Christians are very easy to offend, and others are very hard to offend. Why is that?

Some people seem full of grace and humility and it takes a lot to offend them. They are quick to think the best rather than the worst and to bear with minor annoyances and weaknesses. You have to work hard to offend them!

Other people seem quick to think the worst and quick to take offence at every small thing. They take offence when none is intended, and people tiptoe nervously around their oversensitive egos, trying not to upset them. I need to look at myself and make sure I am not being that difficult person.

Yes, I do need to be clear that my brother has actually *sinned* against me before I go and try to show him his fault. It may be that the problem is, in fact, on my side.

It is also possible to have a fault-finding, critical spirit which enjoys scoring points and putting others down in order to boost my own pride. I need to be very careful here, too. I need to be dealing radically with my own sin. I need to be taking the 'planks' out of my own eyes before I start trying to help my brother remove any 'specks' which are in his (Matt. 7:3–5).

But, having said all that, I do not love my brother if I leave him in his sin. If he has sinned, I must go and help him come to repentance. For without repentance he cannot receive forgiveness from God or from me. Forgiveness can be offered. But it cannot be received without repentance. Forgiveness is a transaction with two

I do not love my brother if I leave him in his sin

sides. Both sides need to do their part for forgiveness to reach its goal of a restored relationship.

Sadly, there will be situations where an offender cannot or will not receive the forgiveness I want to offer. Maybe that person remains unrepentant. Maybe making contact with the offender is impossible or unwise. What then? Jesus calls on me to forgive everyone who sins against me. What will that look like in these difficult situations?

I need to decide to forgive. I need to choose an attitude of heart which is willing to hand over my forgiveness. As I think about that other person, I need to see myself as 'putting out my hand' to them. In my heart I need to keep my offer of forgiveness stretched out to them. I need to do this whether or not they take it. I need to remain willing to hand over my forgiveness should that person ever be willing and able to repent and receive it.

In such sad circumstances, forgiveness cannot reach what might be called its 'full flowering'. The aim of forgiveness is a restored relationship and this goal cannot be fulfilled if the other party does not respond. But I can and must still do my half of the transaction of forgiveness in so far as I am able. I must, at the very least, keep the 'open hand of forgiveness' stretched out towards that person as I think of them in my heart.

4. Forgiveness is a decision of the will. You choose to do it.

We need to choose to forgive just as the king chose to cancel the debt.

This is really important to grasp. I think we tend to think of forgiveness as an emotion. But the Bible talks about forgiveness as a decision of the will. It is not trying to whip up a certain feeling. It is making a deliberate choice. You can choose to do it. Or you can choose not to do it. That is why we can be commanded to forgive. Emotional change may follow, but forgiveness itself is a decision.

The Bible always speaks about forgiveness in a 'just do it' kind of a way. Jesus said, 'when you stand praying, if you hold *anything* against *anyone*, forgive him' (Mark 11:25, my italics). Just do it. Decide to stop holding on to that file of sin. Give it up.

Jesus' words there underline that the heart of forgiveness is a decision made in the heart. That decision will flow out into all kinds of changed behaviour. But forgiveness itself is a decision made in the heart. Jesus pictures someone standing praying. As this person is praying, he realizes that he is holding something against another in his heart. Jesus says, 'if you hold *anything* against *anyone*' (my italics). Here Jesus is stressing the universal nature of His command to offer forgiveness. *Whatever* has happened, *whether or not* the other person is sorry, Jesus says, 'forgive him'. Change the attitude of your heart towards that other person. Do it right then and there, as you stand praying. Decide in the privacy of your heart to stop holding that grudge. Let it go. Forgive that other person. Just do it.

Sometimes people say, 'I'm not sure if I have forgiven that person properly because I still wrestle with the whole thing again sometimes.'

What would you say to someone who said that? We need to explore this issue more deeply so that we think clearly about it. For it is vital that we understand this.

Think for a moment about what it means to become a Christian. On 'Day One' we repent. We repent of our sins and decide to live with Jesus as Lord and Saviour. What happens then? Do we instantly become perfect? No more battles with sin? Of course not. Paul wrote to the Christians in Colossae, *'just as* you received Christ Jesus as Lord, *continue* to live in him' (Col. 2:6, my italics). In other words, the decision we make on 'Day One', we are to live out every day. Every day I am to make every effort, with God's help,

Each day I need to keep turning away from sin

to mould my life to the decision I made on that first day. Each day I need to keep turning away from sin. Yes, I will fail, again and again. But every time I fail, I am to come back to Christ for forgiveness and keep going, following Christ as Lord. Every day I am to put to death my old nature. Every day I am to put on my new self (Col. 3:5–14).

And the decision to forgive is exactly like that. In fact it is part of it. I make the decision to forgive once, and then each day I need to make every effort to mould my life to that decision. I need to pray for God to help me to do that. Every day I need to put to death my old nature which wants to harbour a grudge and to pay that person back. And I need to put on my new nature. Time and again I may need to interrupt my own thought processes and remind myself, 'No, I am not going to think like that. I am not going to do that. I am not going to say that, because I have decided to forgive that person.'

5. Forgiveness is like a key to a door. Its aim is to open the way to a restored relationship.

The context of Jesus' story in Matthew 18 is reconciliation within the church family. Forgiveness is never an end in itself. Jesus died to bring us forgiveness. But He didn't die so we could then file our 'Forgiveness Certificate' away in a bottom drawer somewhere and go on ignoring God. Christ died for sins to bring us to God (1 Pet. 3:18). Christ died to end the divide and restore the relationship.

Our forgiveness of others should have the same aim. We need to take steps in that direction in so far as it is possible.

Sadly, reconciliation is not always possible. Situations can be messy and complex. The person may have died. We may have lost touch. They may not be a trustworthy person, so the kind of relationship it is wise to have with them may be limited by that. But within all those constraints, the aim of forgiveness is always to open the way to a restored relationship, and we need to head in that direction in so far as we are able. Exactly what that will look like in practice will be different in different situations. In his book, *The Peacemaker*,* Ken Sande gives much helpful and practical advice about how to pursue reconciliation. A restored relationship is a wonderful experience. It is worth pursuing.

So, we have looked at what forgiveness is. And at how our forgiveness is to follow the pattern of God's forgiveness of us. But Jesus' story here in Matthew 18:21–35 doesn't just help us understand what forgiveness is. The main aim of Jesus' story is to help us forgive when we don't want to.

Questions to think about and discuss ...

Look again at Jesus' story in Matthew 18:21–35.

- **What is the big point Jesus is making in the story?**

- **What strikes you about the story?**

- **What are the shocks in the story?**

---

* Sande, K., *The Peacemaker* (Grand Rapids, MI: Baker, 2004).

How Jesus' Story Helps Us to Forgive

What Jesus does here in this story is to take the situation of the Christian who won't forgive and put it on a stage. He pulls the camera back, as it were, and says, 'Look. Look at what you are saying when you say you won't forgive that person in your church who asks for your forgiveness.'

Here are five lessons from this story to help us when we are finding it hard to decide to forgive someone.

I. Change the film

As we have seen, when we are wronged, very often we

keep playing the film of what has been done to us in our head. And the more we play it, the more it whips us up into resentment and bitterness. So, change the film.

In His story, Jesus focuses our attention *first* on the free forgiveness we ourselves have received from God. The first focus in the story is the massive debt which the king cancels for the first servant. This is a picture of the mercy God has shown us in Christ. That is the film we need to keep playing to ourselves. Focus your attention there. Stop focusing on what has happened between you and your brother, and look first at what has happened between you and God through Christ's death. Meditate on that. Change the film.

2. Get a big screen

When we are wronged, what has been done to us often looms very large in our minds. It can fill our horizons. What Jesus is saying here is, get a sense of scale. Get a big screen, as it were. See the vastness – the vastness of the forgiveness God has given you.

Your offence against God as a sinful human being is off the scale. That is what Jesus is saying here, and He should know. However great the offence your brother has caused you, and it may be very great, it is miniscule in comparison with the offence you have caused God. And Jesus is saying here, 'See that.'

And see just how staggeringly vast is the forgiveness God

has given to you. The king forgave the first servant 10,000 talents. That was an eye-wateringly large sum of money. So large that the servant could never have paid it back, however long and hard he had worked. If that servant had focused on what he had just been forgiven instead of the debt he was owed, how different his response would have been. And Jesus' message is clear. See the scale of what God has done for you. Get a big screen.

3. Get a mirror

The point here is, see who you really are. You are a servant and you too are a sinner. You and the brother who has wronged you are fellow servants and fellow sinners. God is the King, not you. And the only reason you, yourself, are walking around free from the threat of hell is purely God's free grace. It is nothing to do with your own goodness. You were totally unable to pay the debt you owed God. You did not deserve to be forgiven. Look in the mirror and see how small you are.

We need to walk with others with a deep sense of humility. And that should make us hard to offend in the first place, and quick to forgive. As we have seen, those who are the most godly tend to be the hardest to offend. The more we are conscious of our own failings and of God's grace to us, the more we will grow to be generous-hearted with others in their weakness. If we see who we really are, how can we not walk with humility? How can we not learn to be other-person centred rather than touchy and self-engrossed? Get a mirror.

4. Be a channel, not a pond

The first shock of Jesus' story is the vastness of the first servant's debt and of the king's forgiveness. The second shock is that servant's failure to pass on that experience of forgiveness to his fellow servant.

This man has just been written a cheque for millions of pounds and he won't pass on to his fellow servant a handful of £20 notes. We are meant to be shocked. And angry. How could he?

Receiving forgiveness from God is supposed to transform us into people who forgive. Forgiveness is supposed to be like a river which does not stop with us. We aren't supposed to be dammed up, stagnant ponds of grace. God's grace is supposed to flow out through us to transform the church and the world. And this story headlines that for us so we see it really clearly.

Forgiveness is supposed to be like a river which does not stop with us

The first servant had been given the most generous and undeserved experience of forgiveness imaginable. He should have passed on that experience of free forgiveness to his fellow servant. Through Jesus' death, we too have experienced God's wonderful grace and forgiveness. And we are to pass on that experience. We are to forgive those who offend us. 'Forgive as the Lord forgave you,' wrote Paul in Colossians 3:13. Pass it on. So, be a channel, not a pond.

5. Victims need to watch out

This is the final shock of the story. Who ends up being punished? It is the servant who has been wronged. Not his fellow servant who owes him. That is a shock. And it warns us that if we are wronged, we need to watch out. God takes this issue of forgiveness very seriously indeed. As we have seen, it is like the litmus test of genuine faith in Christ. For if we have been forgiven by Christ, we will be willing to forgive.

So, don't play with bitterness and resentment in your heart. Those things are spiritual strychnine. They are poison. If you want to stay safe, make the decision to forgive, and make it quickly.

Questions to think about and discuss ...

- **Why is it that when we are wronged we often have the desire to pay the other person back?**

- **Why is it that we often find it so hard to let things go? Why do we struggle to just forgive?**

But Where is the Justice?

There is something else about this story Jesus told. The story raises a question which is not answered within the story itself. And the question is, 'Where's the justice?' How can the king just rip up the accounts book and act like it doesn't matter? The first servant owed his master a massive amount of money. He must have done a great deal wrong to have run up such a huge debt.

Remember, Jesus' theme in Matthew 18 is forgiving wrongs. So, does sin not really matter to God? Can He just say, 'Oh well, never mind. Let's just forget about it.'?

That is a question this story raises, and it points us forward. Forward to Jesus' death on the cross where that question is answered. For the truth is that God does not 'just forgive'.

There is one other massively important truth about forgiveness which we haven't looked at yet. Earlier we saw five truths about forgiveness from this story Jesus told. But there is a sixth truth about forgiveness which is not contained within the story itself. This story raises the question and points us forward to the answer. But it is only at the cross that we come to understand the sixth truth about forgiveness.

A sixth truth: Forgiveness is only possible because sin is fully and finally paid for

That is what the cross tells us. For sin is not a nothing. It matters. When God forgives me, when He forgives you, He does so because our sin is paid for. Jesus paid for it as He died on the cross. He was paying the price for our sin, bearing the punishment our sin deserved.

God's forgiveness is like the NHS in this regard – it is free at the point of delivery, but it is massively costly to provide. Sin is not paid for by us, but it *is* paid for. Writing about the cross, Isaiah prophesied, 'the LORD has laid on him', that is, on Jesus, 'the iniquity of us all' (Isa. 53:6). Paul wrote to the Christians at Colossae, God 'forgave us all our sins' (Col. 2:13). As Jesus died, God was 'nailing' the record of our sins to the cross (Col. 2:14). Forgiveness is only possible because sin is paid for.

So, the reaction we often have when we are sinned against that there ought to be a payback of some kind – that struggle we have to just forgive, to just let it go – there is a rightness in that reaction.

Yes, there will be all sorts of sinfulness and selfishness mixed up in our reactions, too. But the pain we experience, the anger at the wrongness of what has been done, the feeling that there ought to be a payback for sin, that *something* should happen – those things are echoes in us of the justice of God, in whose image we are made. For it is true, sin is not a nothing. The wrongness of a sinful act may well continue to make us righteously angry. For sin matters. It cannot just be swept under the carpet. All sin must be paid for.

The wrongness of a sinful act may well continue to make us righteously angry

But God's Word speaks to us very clearly and decisively when we feel we want payback. In effect God says to us, 'Know your job.'

Know Your Job

Yes, all sin must be dealt with. But God's Word tells us that it is not *our* job to deal with sin. That is God's job. When we are sinned against in our personal relationships, it is as if God asks us to stand aside and let Him deal with it, to pass the file to Him. It is God's world and all sin is first and foremost an offence against Him. So, when someone wrongs me, I need to remember that God is that person's maker and judge, not me. God cares about sin, all sin, a great deal more than we do. And all sin will be fully and finally paid for. God will make sure of that. Nothing will be ignored or swept under the carpet.

There are only two places where sin is fully and finally dealt with. One is the cross. And the other is hell. Either my sin will be laid on Christ in His death, or I will pay for it myself in hell. But it *will* be paid for. We can trust God to deal with all sin with perfect justice. As Abraham said about God, 'Will not the Judge of all the earth do right?' (Gen. 18:25).

We can trust God to deal with all sin with perfect justice

When God calls on me to forgive, He is not calling on me to rip up the file of that person's sin. He is asking me to let go of it and give it to Him to deal with. He is saying, 'Pass it to Me. Leave it with Me. You can trust Me to deal with it.' We find it hard to do that. But actually God is inviting us to walk in a pathway of great blessing. He is inviting us to give up carrying around the burden of that file, which pulls us down towards bitterness.

Someone said, 'Unforgiveness is the poison we drink, hoping someone else will die.' It is true. Refusing to forgive someone is spiritual suicide. The other person may not even realize I am nurturing a grudge against them. It may not affect them. But it will certainly affect me. It will twist and damage me inside as bitterness takes root. To refuse to forgive is to turn my back on God's transforming grace. It is to declare myself to be outside of God's forgiveness. It is spiritual suicide. God does not want that for me.

> Unforgiveness is the poison we drink, hoping someone else will die

But there is more. This is not just about me. This is about the other person, too. This is about relationships. In calling on me to forgive, God is also handing me the key which can open the door to a restored relationship, and all the joy that brings.

Thinking Personally

Let's apply these truths to personal situations. Think for a moment. Who has sinned against you? You know them. I don't. But I do know this – that person will either be a Christian or a non-Christian. That person will either be a follower of Christ or an enemy of Christ. There is no third category.

If they are a Christian, you need to see that person as your brother or your sister 'for whom Christ died', as Paul described Christians in Romans 14:15. If they are a Christian, they will be repenting of sin and trusting Christ. And their sin, including their sin against you, will be paid for by Jesus Christ in His death.

You might ask, what about if they are an *unrepentant*

Christian? An unrepentant Christian is an oxymoron. It is a contradiction in terms. Jesus makes the point in the passage just before our story that a Christian who refuses to repent of sin is actually no Christian at all (Matt. 18:17).

What about if the person who has wronged you is not a Christian?

God's Word to us here is this – do not hit back yourself. Paul says in Romans, 'Do not take revenge, my friends, but leave room for God's wrath, for it is written: "It is mine to avenge; I will repay," says the Lord' (Rom. 12:19). In other words, God is saying, 'You can trust Me to be the perfect judge. I am in possession of all the facts. I will punish sin. I will give that person exactly what they deserve on the last day.'

Do not hit back yourself

So, God will deal with all sin. At the end of the day, every person will either turn out to be your brother or sister for whom Christ died, or they will turn out to be Christ's enemy who will face Christ as Judge on the last day. All sin will either be paid for by Christ or by the sinner themselves in hell. But don't you do it; don't you try to do it now. It is not your job.

So, what is our job? What is our job when we are sinned against?

Our job is to preach the gospel by our life as well as by our lips.

When you forgive, you are giving a practical demonstration of the gospel

Yes, we must explain the gospel in words. But when you forgive that person who has sinned against you, you are giving them a first-hand practical demonstration of the gospel. You are showing them what the gospel of grace means. For who does God forgive? Whoever repents and believes. *Whoever*. No limitations. And we are to forgive like that.

What about the person who doesn't repent? For of course not everyone who sins against us is sorry. How should we respond to those who hurt us and oppose us and who aren't sorry at all? The answer is – just like God does in the gospel. God gave His Son for a world which stood in rebellion against Him: 'For God so loved the world that he gave his one and only Son' (John 3:16).

In the face of the world's sinful rebellion against Him, God made the first move. And what a costly move it was. God did not wait till we were sorry. It was 'while we were still sinners' that Christ died for us. It was 'when we were God's enemies' (Rom. 5:8,10).

God gave. So I, if I am a Christian, need to give, too. And I am to give first, before my enemy repents. I am to do good to those who are unrepentant. I am to show in my life that God so loved the unrepentant world that He gave.

Paul wrote, 'If your enemy is hungry, feed him; if he is thirsty, give him something to drink' (Rom. 12:20). Don't just resist the desire to pay your enemy back, but go out of your way to help him.

Paul's words there about enemies show us how we should express our forgiveness to someone who is unrepentant. Your enemy is someone who seeks to hurt you. Maybe they have hurt you already. Your enemy is, by definition, an unrepentant person. In your heart you need to forgive this person who is against you. But unless your enemy repents, you cannot actually hand this forgiveness over to him or her. As we have seen, a person cannot receive forgiveness unless they repent. Without this giving and receiving of forgiveness, true reconciliation cannot take place. So, how should we treat such an unrepentant person who does not acknowledge and turn from their sin? What will be the outward sign of a forgiving heart in this situation? We need to treat the offender with a grace which mirrors God's grace to us. Paul's words about enemies echo the teaching of the Lord Jesus Himself.

We need to treat the offender with a grace which mirrors God's grace to us

Jesus said, 'Love your enemies, do good to those who hate you, bless those who curse you, pray for those who ill-treat you' (Luke 6:27–28). We are to put our hands out to help them. We do this not to affirm them in their sin; we need to make clear to them, as humbly as we can, that we do not approve of their sin. But we also need to preach the gospel of grace to them in our actions as well as our words, to help them to come to repentance.

Two Final Thoughts...

Every time we are sinned against, there, in that situation, God is giving us an invitation and an opportunity.

The invitation

The invitation is to come again to the cross of Jesus.

When I feel pain and anger at being sinned against, God is speaking to me about what sin is and what sin does. God is showing me again the seriousness and the destructive power of sin. This experience is like a window on the heart of God and the cross of Christ. God is inviting me to see something of the pain *my* sin causes *Him*. He is calling me to come close and to see how much Jesus loved me in bearing the price for my sin.

The opportunity

God is also giving me, giving you, the opportunity to hand the gospel to that other person in the way I respond.

When someone sins against me, it is as if they give me a file of their offences against me. This file is heavy and cumbersome. I can choose to carry it around. I can use it as a barrier between us. I can use it as a weapon to try to hit that person back. I can pore over it, dwelling on every detail as bitterness grows inside me. Or I can decide to hand that file over to Christ and to leave it with Him, trusting Him to deal with that sin.

If I am a Christian, I have something else in my hands, too. I have the gospel of God's grace to me in Christ. And when I am sinned against, I can take that gospel of grace and I can choose to hand it on to that person who has sinned against me. How I respond can model the gospel of grace to them, to draw them to Christ, or to sustain them in Him.

Imagine you are holding a copy of a Gospel in your hands now, and think of the person who has sinned against you.

Will you hand over the Gospel?

Will you hand over the Gospel to that person in how you respond? Or will you refuse to hand it over? Will you decide to hold on to that Gospel and just keep God's grace for yourself? For that is what we do when we refuse to forgive.

Jesus warns us starkly that if we refuse to pass the gospel

on, we show that it is not truly ours and we will receive none of its blessings.

With God's help, we are to be channels of His grace, to transform His world. 'Forgive, as the Lord forgave you.' Make the decision. Just do it.

A Prayer for God's Help to Forgive

'Blessed is the man [or woman] whose sin the Lord will never count against [them]' (Rom. 4:8).

Heavenly Father, thank You for Your free and full forgiveness in Christ. Please help us to forgive as we have been forgiven.

In Jesus' name we pray.

Amen.